DAWN

Ephemeral Darkness to Eternal Light

AALIYAH PARVEZ

BLUEROSE PUBLISHERS
India | U.K.

Copyright © Aaliyah Parvez 2025

All rights reserved by author. No part of this publication may be reproduced, stored in a retrieval system or transmitted in any form or by any means, electronic, mechanical, photocopying, recording or otherwise, without the prior permission of the author. Although every precaution has been taken to verify the accuracy of the information contained herein, the publisher assumes no responsibility for any errors or omissions. No liability is assumed for damages that may result from the use of information contained within.

BlueRose Publishers takes no responsibility for any damages, losses, or liabilities that may arise from the use or misuse of the information, products, or services provided in this publication.

For permissions requests or inquiries regarding this publication, please contact:

BLUEROSE PUBLISHERS
www.BlueRoseONE.com
info@bluerosepublishers.com
+91 8882 898 898
+4407342408967

ISBN: 978-93-6783-506-7

Cover design: Yash Singhal
Typesetting: Namrata Saini

First Edition: January 2025

To those ensnared in the darkness…

may you find your way back into the light

Foreword

A Letter from a Sister

Every night, having said our goodnights and being tucked into bed, I'd await our 3 year old poetess' curious voice that said,

"Zara, can I tell you a story?"

And night after night, just like clockwork, there would once be "a rabbit that stole a carrot", then as rabbits do, venture out "to the market with mama rabbit" to buy... you guessed it! More CARROTS!

Then, she was 7, penning down poems in a little black diary about trees and ladybugs and life as she knew it; until one day they weren't just amusing words written down by a little girl looking at life through rose coloured glasses- they were so much more.

Aaliyah Parvez is the one I have the delightful pleasure of calling my younger sister. Be that as it may, she is the one I call to be my sanctum in my mayhem, she is the one that helps me fight my inner demons and believe me there have been plenty. Her unique charm so evidently consistent in her work consists of reigniting the spirits of anyone who has the pleasure of her reassurances.

Dawn: Ephemeral Darkness to Eternal Light will be your sanctum in whatever mayhem you find yourself traversing through. It is a pocket guide to despair. You might be thinking that this is quite an absurd description for a book I am quite literally trying to sell to you! However, we find ourselves living in a world of toxic positivity where we are almost made to believe that we simply must be happy- content at all times. By contrast, when we are in fact not happy, we must then simply pretend for why would we ever acknowledge our struggles!? Why would we ever let them show? It is not as though we all have hard times..right?

This anthology is therefore a guide to despair, navigating through the darkest of abysses to emerge into your Dawn. I do not claim for it to be a roadmap nor a pair of shoes you step into- whereby one size fits all. However, I promise you this- Dawn will meet you at your horizon, wherever that might be. It will hold your hand like my sister has always held mine and gently tug you toward the gleaming sunrise all whilst being the perfect little escape as you make your way through some treacherous tunnels of life along the way. Remember, it is okay to take your time. Remember, it is indeed okay to not be okay.

Love,

Zara xx

P.S. My dearest Aaliyah, I always knew it in my heart that enduring the same story 143637 times over would someday be worth it. This is it! So very proud of you my bunny rabbit x

Preface

Dawn: Ephemeral Darkness to Eternal Light chronicles a transformative journey from the haunting depths of darkness to the illuminated promise of a new tomorrow – one filled with hope and transcendence.

The poems in the first half of this anthology—*Darkness*—are born from a period when I found myself trapped in a shadowed state of mind. The world appeared fractured beyond repair, filled with misery and pain. I was convinced it wasn't me who saw the world through a broken lens; it was the world itself that was irrevocably broken. This belief left me stranded in a relentless cycle of melancholy and fear. Each day felt like an attempt to move forward, yet I remained shackled by self-doubt, irrational fears, and an unwillingness to try—afraid that failure would only deepen my wounds. I existed in the grip of my past, unable to embrace the present, questioning my worth and my very purpose.

Then, one day, something shifted. A glimmer of light pierced through the cracks in my broken soul. That moment marked the beginning of my healing—a gradual unraveling of fear, doubt, and despair. Slowly, I found the courage to hope again, to believe in myself and in the possibility of joy. The poems in the second half—*Light*—are a testament to this awakening. They stand as a reminder that, no matter how infinite the darkness may feel, it is never eternal.

Hard times pass. What is broken can be mended. The journey may be arduous, and the darkness overwhelming, but light always finds a way in. This book is my promise to you: there is hope, even in the bleakest of moments. And when the light returns, it illuminates not just the world around you but the strength within you.

About the Author

Aaliyah Parvez, 16, is a small-town girl from the picturesque hills of Shillong, now thriving amidst the energy of Mumbai as a Grade 11 student. Ever since she discovered the magic of the English language, she has been captivated by literature and poetry, using words to articulate her deepest emotions. She is a passionate lover of literature weaving words into vivid tapestries that express the depths of her emotions.

An ardent lover of the cosmos, Aaliyah is an astrophile who draws inspiration from the mysteries of celestial bodies and the infinite universe. She is also a talented musician who finds joy in playing the piano and guitar, singing, and immersing herself in music. Driven by ambition and a desire to grow, Aaliyah strives to become the best version of herself, never settling for anything less than excellence.

While she has been writing poetry for years, Dawn: Ephemeral Darkness to Eternal Light marks her debut anthology. Through this collection, she shares her personal journey of resilience and hope, inviting readers to join her in finding light even in the darkest of moments.

Acknowledgement

I may have been the one to weave these verses together, hoping to etch my emotions into words that resonate with others. But it is only through the unwavering support of a few cherished souls that these verses, these words, and these emotions have transformed into the pages of this book today. To those who stood by me during my darkest and most vulnerable moments, to those who believed in me when I struggled to believe in myself, to those who found light within me even when I felt lost in the shadows—here's to you.

To my mother, who has been my inspiration and my safe haven. You encouraged me to dream and gave me the courage to pursue those dreams. I still remember the first diary you gifted me for writing poetry and the pride in your eyes when I wrote my first poem. I held onto your words that day: *"My daughter will one day be a poet."* A decade later, here I am—a poet, because you believed in me even before I believed in myself.

To my father, whose wisdom and strength have shaped me into the person I am today. I remember the very first time you read me the poem *"Invictus" by William Ernest Henley*, I fell in love with poetry. Your life lessons and advice, though I may have resisted them at times, have always guided me. You've taught me to rise above fear and to find faith even in the direst of times. Thank you for your resilience and for always being there for me.

To my sister, Zara, my biggest cheerleader and the first to hear the verses I write. You have always been my anchor, my confidant, and my best friend. From the silly games of childhood to the deep conversations of today, your presence has been my constant. Your unwavering belief in me has been a beacon of strength. You are talented, intelligent, beautiful, and above all, a good person. Please never change. You make me proud every single day. *I love you, always and forever.*

To my friends, who have been my pillars of support. To the ones I've laughed with and cried with, the ones who have never judged me and loved me for me. To those who lifted me when I felt low, who accepted me for who I am—I am forever grateful. Your love and encouragement have been an integral part of my journey.

Nokrikchira Sangma, the one with whom I always feel at home, the greatest friend I could've asked for.

Samriddhi Regmi my best friend from the very first day, thank you for always being there for me and believing in me.

Anandita Nair, you are one of the most amazing people I've met, though it's been less than a year since I met you, it feels like I've known you forever. Thank you for always giving me the right advice.

Ananya Daga, the one who encouraged me to publish my poetry. You are the most genuine friend anyone could ask for, you inspire me each day and I appreciate you so very much.

A heartfelt thanks to my editor, *Nathan Godson*, for treating my work with care and for providing thoughtful, constructive criticism that strengthened this book. I appreciate all the contributions you have made and I appreciate your encouragement.

To the team at *BlueRose Publishers*, thank you for your incredible support and guidance. You made the journey from manuscript to book a smooth and joyful experience, and I am deeply grateful.

Finally, *to my teachers*–those who first taught me the alphabet and later guided me to analyze and appreciate the beauty of poetry and prose. To my primary school and high school English teachers *Ms Doreen Clara Lyngdoh, Ms Lavinia Kordor Rani, Ms Anita Chakravarty, Ms Sabita Paul, Ms Easterla Badwar* and and to my current English teachers *Mr Maxim MacDonald* and *Ms Shweta Rastogi*, your lessons laid the foundation for my growth, and your encouragement has been an enduring gift. I owe so much of this moment to your wisdom and kindness.

To everyone who played a part in making this book a reality, know that my gratitude for you is boundless. This book stands as a testament to your faith in me, and I hold each of you close in my heart.

Contents

Requiem ..1

Ephemeral Darkness

Ten Thousand Parts ..5

The Call of the Dark ..6

The End ..7

Left in Ruins ..8

Wonderland ..9

Untitled ..10

Façade ..11

Trapped ..12

The Note She Wrote to Herself ..13

Eternal Light

New Beginnings ..17

It's Alright ..18

True Love ..19

Renaissance ..20

Through the Storm ..22

Hold On ..23

The Dreamer ..25

Elysian ..26

Requiem

[In Memory of My Grandmother- My Guardian Angel]

You'll always have my blessings.
Five words you always said to me.
And now that you're gone,
The house feels so empty.

You always believed in me even when I didn't believe in myself,
But now all I have is a picture of you in a frame on a shelf.
I miss your beautiful smile,
And I miss the time we shared
I miss you so much, it just isn't fair.

You taught me kindness, in a world filled with cruelty,
You are the definition of genuine beauty.
Even though you're gone
I can feel you all around.
I feel your blessings and I feel your love.
I promise I'll make you proud,
As you look down from above.

You'll always have my blessings.
Five words engraved in my heart.

Ephemeral Darkness

Ten Thousand Parts

Happiness saw me and said she'd never return,
So, I just sat there helplessly and watched all my dreams burn.
The only thought on my mind,
Was how to leave this all behind.
I tried to ignore all the despair,
But my heart was broken, beyond repair.
My joy stolen, not an ounce of hope left.
Alas, no one would report such a theft.
No one to repay me for what I had lost,
No restitution, no cost.
All I had left was a broken heart, a shattered soul,
Ten thousand parts of what once was whole.

The Call of the Dark

The darkness is calling out my name
I hear the echoes, but something's changed
The allure of darkness has grown so strong
But for once, being drawn to it doesn't feel so wrong.
For once I don't feel the need to fight,
I'm ready to let go of the light

I welcome the darkness with open arms,
I surrender to its charm,
My body and mind are at ease,
My heart and soul have finally found peace.
I let the darkness consume me whole,
I give to it my mind, body and soul.
I spread my wings to fly
For I am no longer scared to die.

The End

I don't claim to know much
But there is one thing I am most certain of:
The happy times are gone my friend
We are one step closer now, to the end.

Hush now, you needn't fear
You needn't let your eyes pool with tears
It's finally time to bid farewell
To this world where we did dwell.

Let go of all that is weighing you down
Surrender to the forces you feel all around.
We've never seen such a sight.
Surrender and let yourself be pulled into the light.
I hope your pain will ease,
I hope we'll find eternal peace.

Left in Ruins

A million different voices telling her a million different things
It's getting so loud, her ears start to ring
She knows in her heart that she did her best
But now that doesn't matter, she's failed the test.

The voices of oppression discrediting her success
One who used to be so perfectly put together, now an utter mess
She's a monster, an abomination, a complete disgrace
All because of the opiniated beings; the human race.
She'll never know the feeling of being appreciated, being loved
Because nothing she'll ever do will ever be enough

No matter how hard she'll try
She'll always end up with tears in her eyes
The world will beat her down
Until she doesn't make a sound
Tarnish her self esteem
Destroy her ability to dream
Because that's the specialty of our united, beautiful human race.
To discourage, belittle and disgrace

Wonderland

I just want somebody
        to hold my hand
And take me far away
        to wonderland

To a place that's filled with magic,
Some place where life doesn't seem so tragic

Just take me where the White Rabbit,
        Mad Hatter,
        and Cheshire Cat dwell,
And I'd gladly bid this world farewell.

Untitled

A mind filled with fear,
And eyes full of tears.

A heart filled with pain,
And a life lived in vain.

You don't want to die sweet child,
You just want the pain to end.

You don't want to lie, I know,
But the truth is simply too hard to comprehend.

Façade

I'll hide my pain, I'll hide my sorrow,
I'll pretend I look forward to tomorrow.
I'll fake a smile, I'll be your hope.
I'll tighten my grip and hold on to the rope.

I'll conceal all my darkest parts
I promise, I'll never ever break your heart.
You'll never meet the demon that hides under my skin
Because exposing you to my true self would be my greatest sin.

Trapped

Always overthinking
But never really thinking,
Assuming the worst
Without finding out what happened first.

Living with this fear that the world's going to come crashing down at me,
Living in denial saying this is not how it's supposed to be,
Think it's time I accept my fate
I've lost everything; now it's too late.

There's no point in regretting the choices I've made
I just wish the pain would all just fade.

The Note She Wrote to Herself

I thought it was getting better,
I thought it would be okay,
But as I write this letter,
I feel like a needle,
Lost in a stack of hay.

I'm trying to figure out what went wrong
If only I had a clue,
It feels like there are lyrics missing from my song,
I just can't figure out why I am so blue.
I need to get a hold of myself,
I need to look ahead.
I can't just be a dusty book on the shelf,
 waiting to be read.

Eternal Light

New Beginnings

There is always a chill in the air
When something fresh is about to start,
The excitement, with a little fear
And then faster and faster beats your heart.

There is a sense of satisfaction with every new beginning
And there is hope with every fresh page we turn,
For once again, we have a shot at winning
And a plethora of valuable lessons to learn.

New people to meet, and places to go
Another chance to learn, to love, and to grow.
A new chapter of the book we call life
So keep writing on, and enjoy the ride.

It's Alright

They say holding on is what makes you strong
But sometimes you've got to let go.
They say you should know how to tell the right from wrong,
But sometimes you needn't know.

Just remember that it's alright
To feel like you've lost the will to fight.
Just know that it's okay
To not be able to find you're needle in a stack of hay.

It's alright, take your time,
Prioritizing your needs is not a crime.
Remember, you are the artist, you get to decide,
The colours you'll choose to paint the canvas that is your life.

True Love

I know not much of true love,
But I know that it exists.
I'm not sure of why, where, or how,
I just know that it lives.

It just seems right that someone out there,
Is meant just for me.
Someone I can call my soulmate, my twin flame,
Someone who is my destiny.

I know not much of true love
But I'm sure that it's enough.
I'm unsure of almost everything
But if there's one thing I'm sure of –
Without a second thought,
It's true love.

Renaissance

She was the kind of girl who would quietly sit in a corner,
-waiting for life to gradually unfold
Until one sudden day,
 the wait grew cold.

Realization had dawned on her
And finally she knew
If you want something, you have to get it
Because it won't come to you

It was almost as though she had awakened
From a long, deep dream
And now she knew exactly what she needed to do to get where she wanted to be

All these years all she did was wait
Stuck in a fragile state.

But now strength was regained,
And she was no longer chained.

Her shackles broken, the cage unlocked
On every door opportunity knocked

She'd been holding herself a prisoner for years
All because of a million little fears

But now strength was regained
And she was no longer chained

Her shackles broken, the cage unlocked
And on every door opportunity knocked
She's finally been freed
She's set out to succeed.

Through the Storm

Don't you lose hope, just keep going on
Hold on tight, you'll get through this storm
You've made it through hard times before,
and this too shall pass
It'll be alright again, 'cause hard times don't last
You'll see the seven colours, after the thunderous rain
And you'll find that the downpour has washed away
your pain
Once again you'll find the strength to stand, walk,
even run
So don't you lose hope
Just keep going on.
Hold on tight, I promise,
You'll get through this storm.

Hold On

When your heart starts to sink
And your soul starts to ache,
When you're standing at the brink
And don't care what's at stake.

When you give up on all your dreams
And let go of all your hope,
When you want to scream
But your tears make you choke.

When you've reached the depths of your despair
And when you're broken beyond repair,
When you know all is lost
And cannot bear to pay the cost.

Look deep into the waters and you'll see
Your reflection staring back telling you to break free.
But in that moment you'll find
A faint voice in your mind
Telling you, "*This is not the end*",
And I promise your heart will mend.

Listen to this faint voice,
Don't focus on the noise.
Because I'll let you in on a little secret my dear friend-
This is rock-bottom but this is not the end.

You've got miles to travel,
And great mysteries to unravel.

So hold on a little longer,
Let yourself heal and become stronger.
And soon you'll find-
You're soaring through the sky.

The Dreamer

She's an ambitious child
And her dreams are oh so wild.
She's got a spark in her eyes,
She's set out to touch the skies.
Her ship has set sail,
She's out to find her holy grail.

You may think she's got it all mapped out
But her head is often filled with doubt,
But she's got courage, she's got faith
And that is why she will not fail.

She's not afraid to face
Any tribulations which may come her way,
She knows in her heart she will succeed
Only if she cries, sweats and bleeds,
She is a dreamer but she doesn't rest
Because she's not willing to settle for anything but the best.

Elysian

Waking up to the smell of petrichor
On a cold winter's morn
Heals the shards of the broken heart
And washes away all things forlorn.

Listening to the symphony of the black bird
As I step into the damp dewy lawn,
Feeling the apricity of the sun on my skin,
Subtle yet so warm.

This morning has the power to make me forget
All my troubles, despair, and regret.
So halcyon, tranquil and serene,
Feels like I've awakened and fallen back into a dream.

www.ingramcontent.com/pod-product-compliance
Lightning Source LLC
LaVergne TN
LVHW061631070526
838199LV00071B/6651